SHARKS!

A Platt & Munk **ALL ABOARD BOOK**™

Library of Congress Cataloging-in-Publication Data
Wilson, Lynn, 1946– Sharks! / by Lynn Wilson ; illustrated by Courtney Studios, Inc. p.   cm. — (All aboard books) Summary: An introduction to the physical characteristics and habits of various species of sharks. 1. Sharks—Juvenile literature.   [1. Sharks.]   I. Title. II. Series.
QL638.9.W56 1992 597'.31—dc20 91-5033
ISBN 0-448-40301-3 (GB) A B C D E F G H I J
ISBN 0-448-40300-5 (pbk) A B C D E F G H I J

SHARKS!

By Lynn Wilson • Illustrated by Courtney

Platt & Munk, Publishers

Long before the time of the dinosaurs, sharks swam in the oceans of the world.

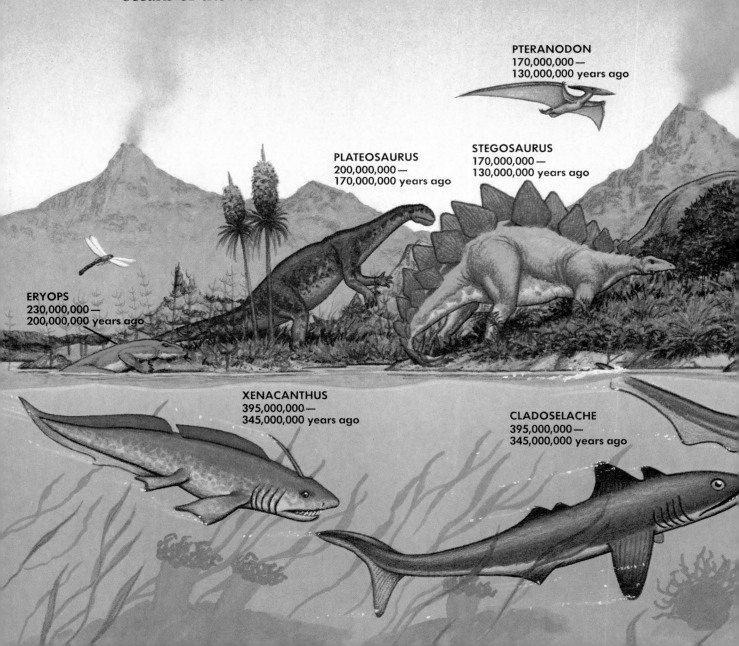

PTERANODON
170,000,000 —
130,000,000 years ago

PLATEOSAURUS
200,000,000 —
170,000,000 years ago

STEGOSAURUS
170,000,000 —
130,000,000 years ago

ERYOPS
230,000,000 —
200,000,000 years ago

XENACANTHUS
395,000,000 —
345,000,000 years ago

CLADOSELACHE
395,000,000 —
345,000,000 years ago

Three hundred million years went by. The dinosaurs came and went. But the sharks survived.

In all those millions of years, sharks have not changed very much.

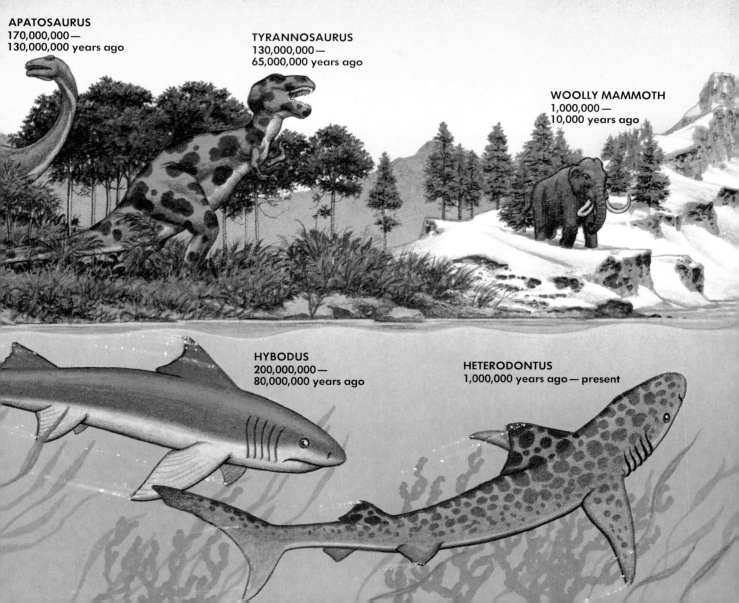

APATOSAURUS
170,000,000 —
130,000,000 years ago

TYRANNOSAURUS
130,000,000 —
65,000,000 years ago

WOOLLY MAMMOTH
1,000,000 —
10,000 years ago

HYBODUS
200,000,000 —
80,000,000 years ago

HETERODONTUS
1,000,000 years ago — present

Today, there are between 250–300 different kinds of sharks. Scientists keep finding new ones.

The whale shark is the biggest fish in the world. It can grow to be more than 40 feet long — longer than a moving van!

Once in a while, a whale shark washes up on a beach. People come from miles away to stare at it. The whale shark looks like a huge sea monster.

The whale shark is huge but harmless. It lives by eating plankton — tiny sea plants and creatures, some so small you need a microscope to see them.

Whale sharks swim near the top of the water. They move so slowly that they sometimes can't avoid bumping into the sides of ships.

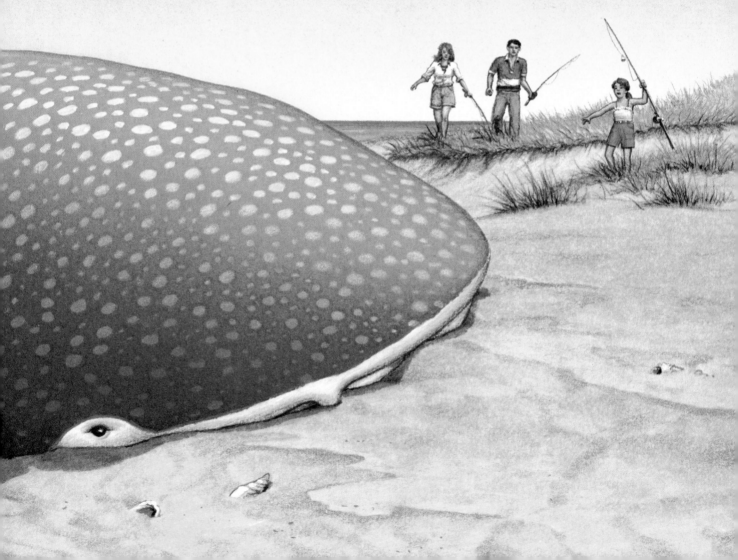

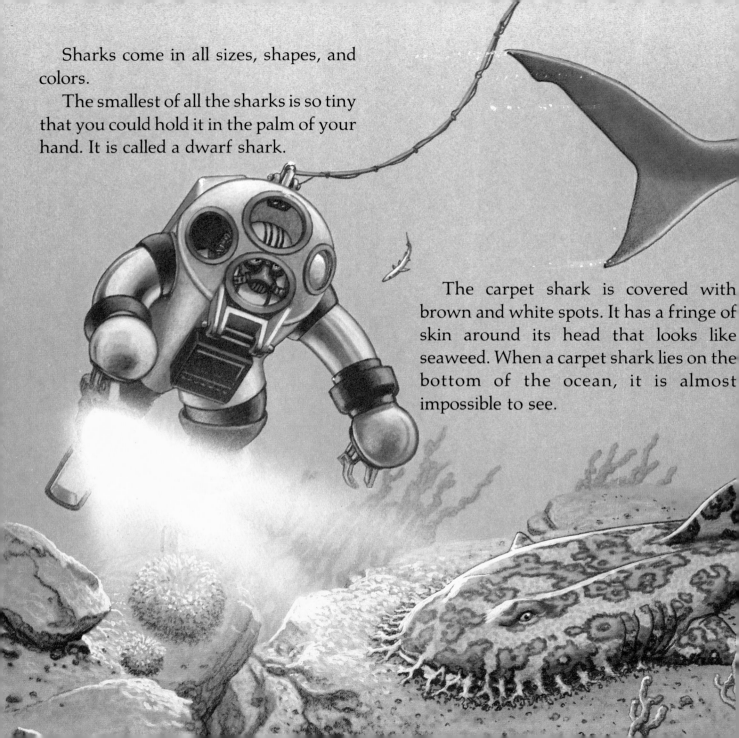

Sharks come in all sizes, shapes, and colors.

The smallest of all the sharks is so tiny that you could hold it in the palm of your hand. It is called a dwarf shark.

The carpet shark is covered with brown and white spots. It has a fringe of skin around its head that looks like seaweed. When a carpet shark lies on the bottom of the ocean, it is almost impossible to see.

The hammerhead shark has a flattened head that looks like a hammer. With slit-like nostrils on either side of its head, the hammerhead can tell which direction an odor is coming from.

Sharks are fish. But they are different from other kinds of fish.

Most fish have flat scales. A shark's scales are hard and pointed, like tiny little teeth. Sharkskin is as tough as leather. If you rub it, it feels rough — like sandpaper.

Sharks are rough on the outside but soft on the inside. Most fish have bones. But a shark's skeleton is soft and rubbery.

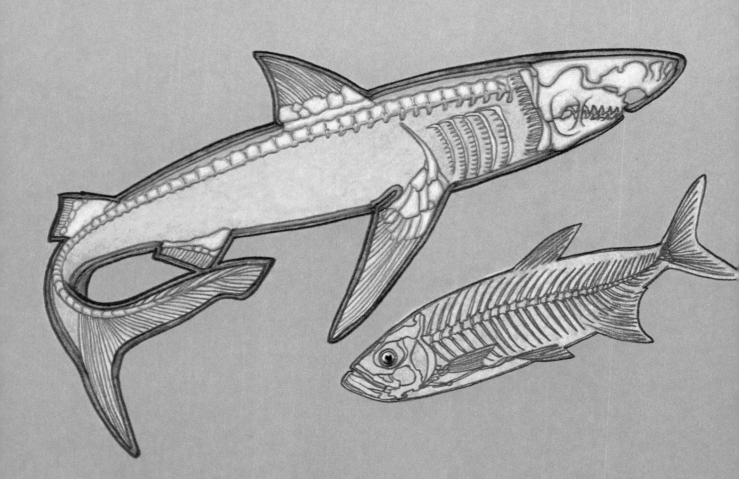

Most fish can float. But not sharks!

Many kinds of fish have swim bladders. The swim bladder is like a little balloon inside the fish's body. As the balloon is filled with air, the fish will rise higher in the water.

A shark has no swim bladder. It flies through the water using its fins like the wings of a plane. If a shark stops swimming, it will sink.

If you look inside a shark's mouth, you will see several rows of teeth, all crowded together. The teeth are as sharp as razors. And there are a lot of them, too.

When a shark bites down hard, sometimes a dozen or so of its teeth in the front row come loose and fall out. The teeth get stuck in whatever the shark is biting.

This doesn't bother the shark at all. The teeth in the next row just move forward. More new teeth grow in the back rows to take their place. A shark goes through about 50 rows of teeth every year!

Most fish lay eggs. But most sharks give birth to live babies. A baby shark is called a pup.

When the mother lemon shark is ready to have her pups, she stays close to the shore. The warm, shallow bays and coral lagoons become the baby sharks' nursery.

The mother lemon shark has about a dozen pups at a time. The pups are pale yellow. They look exactly like their mother.

For the first few months the pups stay in the coral lagoons, where they can hunt for food and remain safe from larger sharks.

From the day it is born, the young shark is a good hunter. Sharks have a very good sense of smell. They can see and hear very well.

Sharks have ears, but you cannot see them. Sharks "hear" through their skin. Some spots on a shark's skin are also very sensitive. The shark can feel vibrations moving through the water. It can tell when a large fish or sea animal is swimming nearby.

Often, sharks just don't seem to be hungry. A shark can go days, even weeks, without eating.

But when sharks do get hungry, they are reported to eat almost anything. Sharks like all kinds of fish.

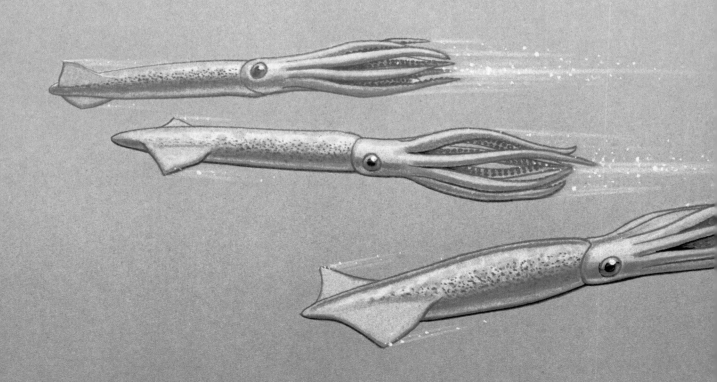

For a big blue shark, a squid can be a tasty meal.

One kind of small shark likes to eat whale blubber. It takes neat little bites out of whales. It is called the cookie cutter shark. Sometimes these sharks eat the rubber parts of submarines because they mistake the sub for a whale!

For a long time, submarine crews wondered what was eating parts of their ships. Then they noticed that they were being followed by a strange green light. The light came from fish. That's how people learned about cookie cutter sharks. These funny-looking little sharks glow in the dark!

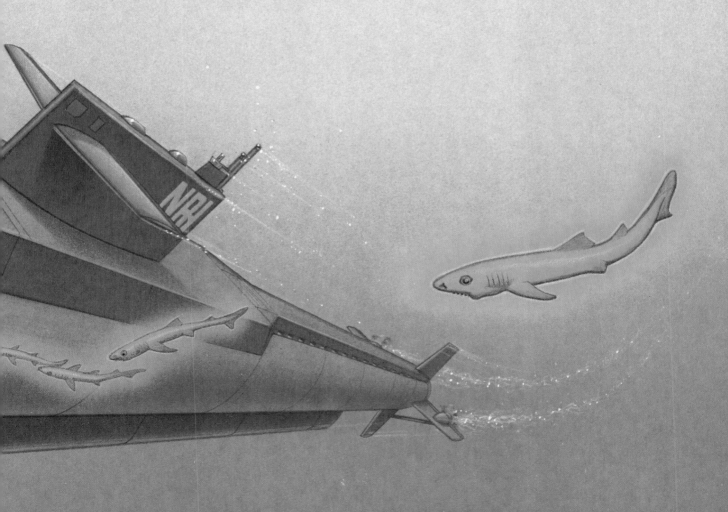

Hungry sharks often swim behind ships. They have learned that a ship will provide lots of food. Sharks are like swimming garbage trucks, ready to scoop up the leftover food and garbage that the sailors throw away.

They will swallow almost anything that falls overboard by accident, too!

When fishermen catch sharks, they can be surprised by what they find inside the sharks' stomachs.

Here are some unusual things that sharks have swallowed:

Empty soda cans.

A car license plate.

Six chickens and a rooster.

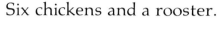

Two pumpkins.

A woman's purse.

A goat.

A raincoat.

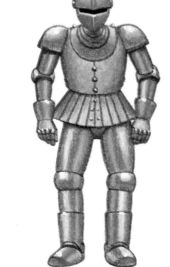

A whole suit of armor.

A reindeer.

Once, a pirate ship was being chased by the British navy. The pirates painted a different name on the side of their ship. That way no one would know it was a pirate ship. But there were some papers that showed the ship's real name. So the pirates put the papers in a wooden chest. Then they dumped the chest overboard.

Weeks later, some fishermen caught a big shark. They found the pirate chest in the shark's stomach.

The papers were still in good shape. The judge read the papers at the pirates' trial. Because of the shark, all the pirates were found guilty!

Once in a while, a hungry shark may even attack a human being. Swimming around sharks is always dangerous. But shark attacks happen more often in books and movies than in real life.

Most kinds of sharks live in the middle of the ocean. They never come near people. Others are too small to be dangerous.

One kind of shark that has attacked people is the great white. Great white sharks grow to be 20 feet long. They are so large that they hunt seals and sea lions.

A baby great white shark is probably about 3-4 feet long when it is born. It may live to be 40 or 50 years old. But we don't know for sure. No one has ever seen a baby great white. Much about this shark's life is still a mystery.

Some people think there are only a few great whites left in the world.

Sharks are often hunted for sport and for food. Sometimes fishermen catch sharks with harpoon guns. But most sharks are caught on long lines. Long lines have many hooks, so it is possible to catch hundreds of sharks in a few hours.

A few kinds of large sharks, like the great white, may already be in danger of dying out. For a long time, most people thought that the world would be a better place without sharks. Today, we know this is not true.

Every year, sharks eat millions of fish — the slow, the careless, the old, the sick. In fact, without sharks, the oceans would be full of sick and dying fish.

With all the things they eat, you might think that sharks would get sick a lot. Strangely enough, they don't.

Sharks are very healthy animals. They do not seem to get cancer, or some other diseases that people get.

Some scientists are studying sharks to find out why. The scientists catch sharks and take samples of their blood. Then they put little metal tags on the sharks and let them go. Sometimes the tagged sharks are caught again, hundreds or even thousands of miles away.

By learning how sharks stay so healthy, the scientists may develop new kinds of medicines for people.

In nature, there are no good or bad animals. The hunter and the hunted each have a role to play.